Saint Nicholas

Text by Mary Joslin
Illustrations copyright © 2003 Helen Cann
This edition copyright © 2004 Lion Hudson

The moral rights of the author and illustrator
have been asserted

A Lion Children's Book
an imprint of
Lion Hudson plc
Mayfield House, 256 Banbury Road,
Oxford OX2 7DH, England
www.lionhudson.com
ISBN 0 7459 4913 4

First hardback edition 2003
First paperback edition 2004
1 3 5 7 9 10 8 6 4 2 0

A catalogue record for this book is available
from the British Library

Typeset in 15/24 BernhardMod BT
Printed and bound in Singapore

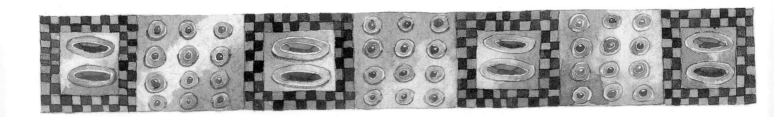

Saint Nicholas
The story of the real Santa Claus

Retold by Mary Joslin

Illustrated by Helen Cann

LION
CHILDREN'S

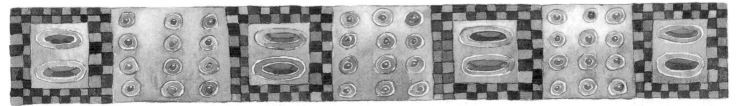

Long ago, in a place called Myra, three sisters lived
with their father. The family had once been wealthy but
had fallen on hard times, and the sisters had to go out
begging.

One winter's day, when the streets were wet with rain,
they were standing shivering on a street corner. Suddenly
they heard the sound of a joyful band playing.

'It's a wedding procession,' said the youngest sister.
'Let's go and see!'

A crowd had already gathered to watch, and the sisters had to stand on tiptoe to catch a glimpse of the bride.

'What a lovely dress she has,' sighed the youngest sister.

'What a wonderful procession she has,' sighed the middle sister.

'What a lovely home she will have with her husband,' sighed the eldest. 'And doesn't he look handsome!'

But then one of the wedding ushers came along.

'Make room for the guests; let them pass,' he ordered.
The sisters had to turn away.

'It's getting dark, anyway,' said the middle sister, 'and my
feet are wet from stepping in puddles. Let's go home.'

Together they trudged through the narrow alleyways. They
did not speak. Each of them was thinking of the wedding
to which they had not been invited. They were too poor for
that. They were so poor that their father could never afford
the dowry that every girl needed if she was to get married.

Back in the shabby dwelling that was their home, they took off their wet shoes and stockings and lit a smoky fire.

Soon their father returned. 'I managed to get a little work today,' he said, 'helping to mend the church roof. Even so, I have not been able to afford much food.'

'Well, we will enjoy sharing it together,' said the eldest sister, trying to sound cheerful. But although they spread the table and each had a bowlful of soup, they did not talk much. Each of the girls was thinking of the great feast that the lucky bride was enjoying in the heart of the town.

Then the fire burnt low and the house grew cold. The sisters left their shoes and stockings by the hearth, their father locked the door and the shutters, and everyone went to bed.

In a great hall in the centre of the town, huge torches burnt to illuminate the wedding festivities. Many wealthy people had gathered in their fine clothes to celebrate the wedding. Now they were eating and drinking, singing and dancing.

Among them walked a plainly dressed man named
Nicholas. He was the leader of the church and had himself
performed the wedding ceremony for the young couple.
Many of the guests knew him as a friend, and indeed
Nicholas tried to be a friend to everyone.

'My dear Nicholas,' called one man. 'Thank you so much for visiting my elderly mother when she was ill and I was away on business. You were so kind! Please accept this little gift with our grateful thanks.'

And he handed over a bag of coins.

A while later, a woman made her way through the crowd to Nicholas. 'My son is so much happier to go to school now that he can read more easily,' she said. 'Thank you so much for helping him to learn his letters. I know you said it was no trouble, but I want to give you a small gift.'

She, too, pressed a purse of coins into Nicholas' hand.

The bride's father saw Nicholas from across the hall and strode over. 'It is a privilege to have you at our daughter's wedding,' he cried. 'We are so pleased you were able to perform the ceremony and ask for God's blessing on our daughter's future. Of course, there is a payment I must give you… and a little extra, which you more than deserve for your kindness.'

Nicholas was given yet another bag of coins, which he slipped into the pockets of his robe.

At midnight, while the party was still in full swing, Nicholas said
his goodbyes. He walked out into the dark streets and found his
way down the narrow alleys to the poorer part of town. At last he
came to the house where the three sisters lived with their father.

'Hmm,' he said, looking up at the building. 'You have no money
to mend your own roof, even though you worked so hard on the
church roof today. Well, maybe that is lucky for me right now.'

Using a cart to help him make the first step, Nicholas
clambered up to the roof and crept along, chuckling like a
mischievous boy.

He steadied himself on the chimney, cold now the fire
was out, and reached in his pockets. 'This should come in
useful to you all,' he said.

One bag of coins. A second. A third.

'Oh dear, that was noisier than
I was hoping,' he muttered to
himself, and he hurried down to
the street and began to run.

The door behind him was flung wide.

'Who's there?' called the father sharply. 'What was that noise?'

Behind him the eldest sister was trying to light a lamp.

'It can't have been a burglar, Father, for we have nothing worth taking. Maybe the noise was soot falling down the chimney.'

'*Something*'s fallen down,' said the youngest sister.

'I can feel things everywhere.'

The lamp spluttered into flame and the eldest sister shone a light.

'It's gold,' whispered the middle sister, in tones of awe. 'Look, gold coins on the hearth, and in our shoes...'

'... and there's even one in the toe of my stocking,' laughed the youngest.

Their father stood behind them, shaking his head in disbelief, his heart filling with gladness.

'Someone has done good things for us,' he said. 'Someone has blessed us.'

At first light, the eldest sister went to the market
to buy food for a feast.

'And I shall come too,' said the middle sister, 'to help
you choose fabric to make yourself a new dress. You'll
need one now because you and Father will have to set
about finding you a husband.'

'Well, you'll need to be thinking of getting married
not long after that,' said the eldest.

'I've got a little longer to wait,' said the youngest,
'so I might have to spend the gold coin in my stocking
on something special just for me!'

As they gathered to eat their first really good meal in a year, their father stood up from the table to make a little speech. 'I don't know who has brought us good fortune today,' he said, 'but yesterday at the church Nicholas told me that all our blessings really come from God. So today we shall thank God for this deed of kindness, and we shall look forward to making our lives happier. Tomorrow, I shall begin to arrange for you, my eldest daughter, to marry a good man, and in time all of you will be brides.'

'What is more,' he said, 'I shall ask Nicholas
to perform the wedding ceremony and to pray for
God's blessing on each of you through all your lives.'

Other titles from Lion Children's Books

Baboushka   *Arthur Scholey and Helen Cann*

Lion Christmas Favourites   *compiled by Lois Rock*

Papa Panov's Special Day   *Mig Holder and Julie Downing*